A Visual Dictionary of the
OLD WEST

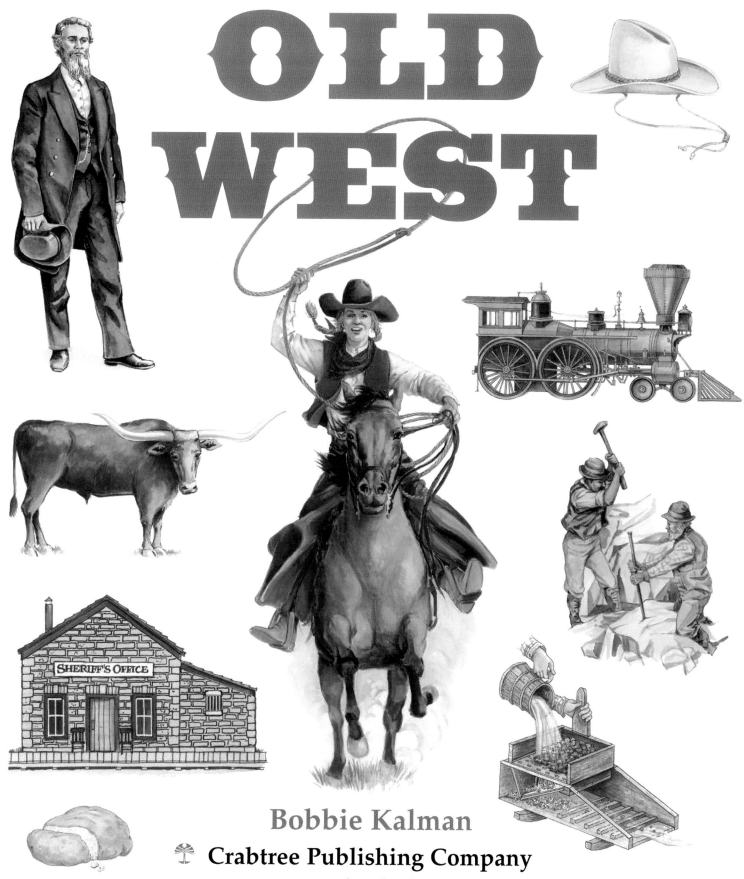

Bobbie Kalman

Crabtree Publishing Company
www.crabtreebooks.com

Crabtree Visual Dictionaries
Created by Bobbie Kalman

For Elfi, my "cowgirl" sister in Vienna.
Finding you has brought great joy to my life. Ich liebe Dich!

Author and Editor-in-Chief
Bobbie Kalman

Editor
Robin Johnson

Research
Crystal Sikkens

Design
Bobbie Kalman
Katherine Berti

Production coordinator
Katherine Berti

Illustrations
Barbara Bedell: front cover (all except cowgirl), back cover (all except train and boot), pages 1 (hat, miners, cradle, and bread), 3 (all except buildings), 4, 5, 9 (saddle, horse, and quirt), 10 (hats), 11 (all except woolies and cowgirl), 12, 13 (top), 14 (trail drive), 15 (all except cowboys), 18 (top), 19 (top), 25 (top left), 26 (bottom), 27, 28 (top), 29, 31 (all except light)
Patrick Ingoldsby: page 31 (light)
Katherine Berti: page 28 (bottom)
Trevor Morgan: page 11 (woolies)
Bonna Rouse: front cover (cowgirl), back cover (train and boot), pages 1 (rancher, cow, building, cowgirl, and train), 3 (buildings), 9 (rope and boot), 10 (cowboy), 11 (cowgirl), 13 (bottom), 14 (cattle), 15 (cowboys), 16, 17, 18-19 (bottom), 20-21, 22, 24, 25 (all except top left), 26 (top), 28 (middle)

Photographs
© iStockphoto.com: pages 25, 30
© 2008 Jupiterimages Corporation: pages 8 (bottom), 9 (right), 15
Bobbie Kalman: pages 5 (bottom), 23 (top right)
Charles M. Russell, *The Whiskey Smugglers*, National Cowboy Hall of Fame, Oklahoma City: page 23 (bottom)
Richard Williams, courtesy of the National Park Service: page 6
© Shutterstock.com: pages 9 (left), 10
Other images by Image Club Graphics

Library and Archives Canada Cataloguing in Publication

Kalman, Bobbie, 1947-
    A visual dictionary of the Old West / Bobbie Kalman.

(Crabtree visual dictionaries)
Includes index.
ISBN 978-0-7787-3503-8 (bound).--ISBN 978-0-7787-3523-6 (pbk.)

    1. Cowboys--West (U.S.)--History--Dictionaries, Juvenile. 2. Cowboys--West (U.S.)--History--Pictorial works--Juvenile literature. 3. Ranch life--West (U.S.)--History--Dictionaries, Juvenile. 4. Ranch life--West (U.S.)--History--Pictorial works--Juvenile literature. 5. West (U.S.)--Social life and customs--Dictionaries, Juvenile. 6. West (U.S.)--Social life and customs--Pictorial works--Juvenile literature. 7. West (U.S.)--History--Dictionaries, Juvenile. 8. West (U.S.)--History--Pictorial works--Juvenile literature. 9. Picture dictionaries--Juvenile literature. I. Title. II. Series.

F596.K3445 2007   j978'.0203   C2007-905680-6

Library of Congress Cataloging-in-Publication Data

Kalman, Bobbie.
    A Visual dictionary of the Old West / Bobbie Kalman.
        p. cm. -- (Crabtree visual dictionaries)
    Includes index.
    ISBN-13: 978-0-7787-3503-8 (rlb)
    ISBN-10: 0-7787-3503-6 (rlb)
    ISBN-13: 978-0-7787-3523-6 (pb)
    ISBN-10: 0-7787-3523-0 (pb)
    1. Cowboys--West (U.S.)--History--Dictionaries, Juvenile. 2. Cowboys--West (U.S.)--History--Pictorial works--Juvenile literature. 3. Ranch life--West (U.S.)--History--Dictionaries, Juvenile. 4. Ranch life--West (U.S.)--History--Pictorial works--Juvenile literature. 5. West (U.S.)--Social life and customs--Dictionaries, Juvenile. 6. West (U.S.)--Social life and customs--Pictorial works--Juvenile literature. 7. West (U.S.)--History--Dictionaries, Juvenile. 8. West (U.S.)--History--Pictorial works--Juvenile literature. 9. Picture dictionaries--Juvenile literature. I. Title. II. Series.

F596.K35 2007
978'.02--dc22
                                    2007037038

Crabtree Publishing Company

Printed in the USA./082019/HF20190711

www.crabtreebooks.com   1-800-387-7650

Published in Canada
Crabtree Publishing
616 Welland Ave.
St. Catharines, Ontario
L2M 5V6

Published in the United States
Crabtree Publishing
PMB 59051
350 Fifth Avenue, 59th Floor
New York, New York 10118

Published in the United Kingdom
Crabtree Publishing
Maritime House
Basin Road North, Hove
BN41 1WR

Published in Australia
Crabtree Publishing
Unit 3 – 5
Currumbin Court
Capalaba QLD 4157

Contents

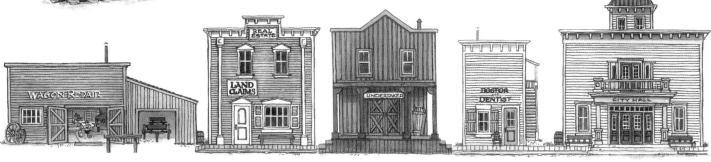

Native nations

Native people lived in North America for thousands of years before people from Europe arrived. There were hundreds of different **nations**, or groups, with different languages, customs, and traditions. Some nations lived in the West. The West was a huge area of land that included flat, grassy areas called **plains** or **prairies**. On the plains, several Native nations lived by hunting buffalo. They did not live in one place. They followed the buffalo wherever the animals roamed. They used buffalo **hides** to make their homes, blankets, and clothing. They ate the meat of the buffalo.

buffalo blanket

*Native people who followed the buffalo lived in tents called **tipis**. Tipis could be taken apart easily and moved from place to place.*

tipi

tipi frame

buffalo

plains

*Some Native nations were farmers. They lived in one place and built **permanent** homes. Some of the plains nations who were farmers built **earth lodges**. Earth lodges were homes made of mud, dirt, and grass.*

*The Southwest was made up of dry deserts. Some nations that lived in the Southwest built homes called **pueblos**. Pueblos were made of **adobe**. (See page 25.)*

pueblo

desert

pueblo

The first Europeans to **settle**, or live, in the West were from Spain. Their **colony** was called New Spain. A colony is an area of land ruled by a faraway country. New Spain included the West, the Southwest, and Mexico. In later times, many other people also settled in the West.

*The Spaniards built **missions**, or religious communities. In the missions, Spanish priests tried to change the religious beliefs of the Native people. They wanted them to become Christians.*

Native people

mission

priest

The Spaniards brought horses and cattle with them. These animals were new to North America. Spanish cowboys, called **vaqueros**, set up ranches all over the West for raising the cattle and horses.

wild horses

vaqueros

wagon

settlers

Many settlers came from the eastern part of North America to find cheap land on which to build homes. They traveled in **wagon trains**. (See pages 16-17.)

wild cattle

cowboy

The cattle that the Spaniards brought grew in number. Soon, there were millions of wild horses and cattle on the plains. The horses and cattle were **rounded up**, or gathered, by cowboys. (See pages 8-15.)

The Great Plains was a large, flat, grassy area of land in the West.

Cattle and horses

The Spanish *vaqueros* did not keep their cattle and horses inside fences. The animals roamed wild all over the plains. Men in eastern North America heard about the wild cattle and came west to set up cattle ranches. Before the cowboys could round up the cattle for the ranches, however, they had to round up wild horses. They trained the horses to help them with the cattle. Cowboys had plenty of work to do!

a bucking wild horse

wild horses

*Rounding up wild horses was hard, but **breaking**, or taming, them was even harder! Wild horses bucked, snorted, kicked, and jumped to get riders off their backs.*

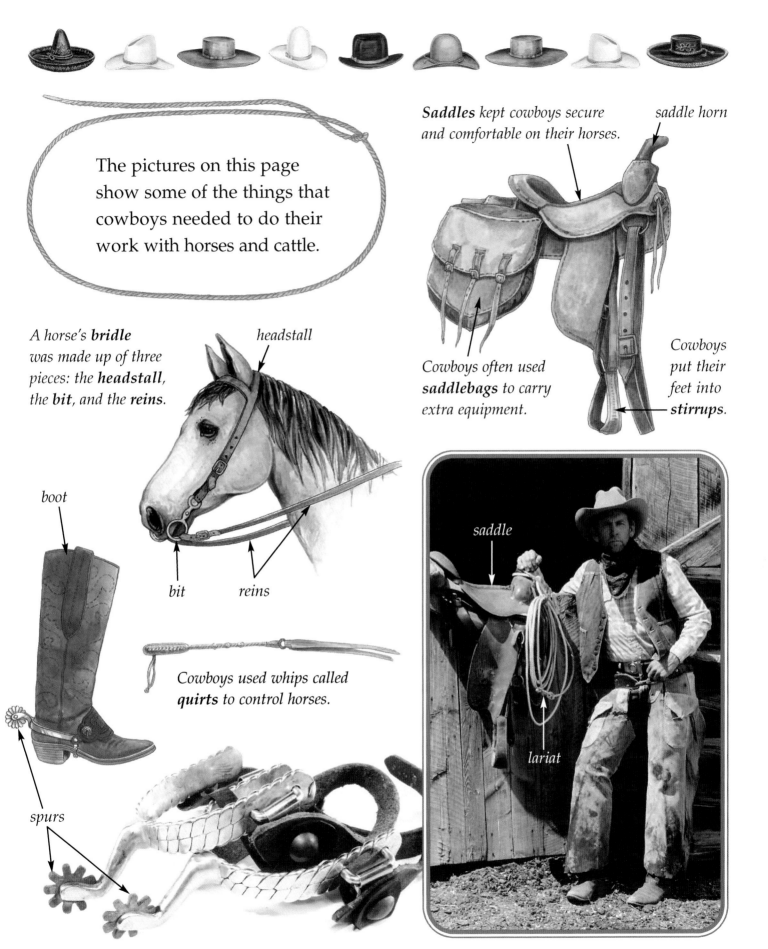

The pictures on this page show some of the things that cowboys needed to do their work with horses and cattle.

Saddles kept cowboys secure and comfortable on their horses.

saddle horn

Cowboys often used *saddlebags* to carry extra equipment.

Cowboys put their feet into *stirrups*.

A horse's *bridle* was made up of three pieces: the *headstall*, the *bit*, and the *reins*.

headstall

boot

bit   reins

Cowboys used whips called *quirts* to control horses.

spurs

saddle

lariat

Spurs were attached to a cowboy's boots. A cowboy touched his spurs against a horse's body to make the horse move.

This cowboy is ready to put his saddle on a horse. His *lariat*, or rope, is attached to the saddle.

Cowboy clothing

Cowboys needed special clothing that was useful, tough, and comfortable. Their clothes had to protect them from the sun, wind, rain, and snow. Each piece of a cowboy's clothing was suited to his job of riding horses and rounding up cattle.

*A cowboy wore a hat with a wide **brim** and a high crown. The hat protected the cowboy's head and neck from the sun. Some styles of cowboy hats are shown on this page.*

sombrero

vaquero

American cowboys learned how to dress from the Spanish vaqueros.

crown → Mexican sombrero

brim

Spanish sombrero

Champie

old-time Texas hat

Dakota

ten-gallon hat

Calgary

Cowboys wore leather leggings called **chaps** over their jeans. The chaps protected their legs and pants from bad weather, thorns, and cattle horns.

chaps

A lariat with a noose at the end is a **lasso**.

Woolies were chaps made from fur or goat hair. Some cowboys wore them for extra warmth in winter.

woolies

lasso

shotgun chaps

front   *back*

batwing chaps

front   *back*

Cowgirls wore the same clothes as those worn by cowboys.

Long leather gloves, called **gauntlets**, protected the hands of cowboys.

Cuffs protected the wrists.

pockets

Cowboys wore **vests** for warmth and for carrying small items.

A cowboy's overcoat had a slit at the back to cover his legs and part of his horse.

11

Cattle ranches

Many cattle ranches opened in the West. Cowboys lived and worked on the ranches. Their jobs included breaking wild horses, rounding up wild cattle, and **branding** the cattle. Branding means burning marks into the hides of cattle to show that a certain ranch owns the animals. Cowboys used **branding irons** to brand the cattle. The branded cattle could then be taken on a **trail drive**.

symbols

branding iron

Cattle were branded with a ranch's symbol.

The picture below shows a large ranch. The **rancher**, or person who owned the ranch, his family, cowboys, horses, and cattle all lived on the ranch.

1. The rancher and his family lived in the **main house**. The main house had a dining room, a big kitchen, and several bedrooms.

2. Horses were kept in the **stables**. Each horse had its own stall with hay for food and straw for bedding.

3. Wild horses were brought to the **corral** to be broken.

4. Windmills were used to pump water out of wells. This ranch had two windmills.

Breaking wild horses was a dangerous job!

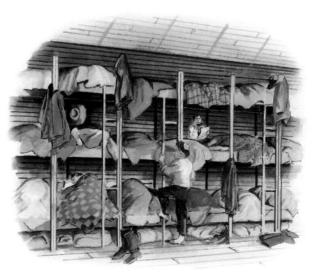

*Cowboys lived in **bunkhouses** such as this one.*

Many cattle ranchers became very wealthy.

13

Life on the trail

There was no refrigeration in the Old West, so cattle like these had to be taken live to cities in the East.

In the early 1800s, many cowboys were hired to **drive**, or guide, cattle. Cowboys drove the cattle to **cattle towns**, or towns that had train stations, so the cattle could be shipped east. This long walk was known as the trail drive. Cowboys who worked on the trail suffered bad weather, bears, and rattlesnakes. They had to work hard to keep the cattle together and to make sure they did not lose any animals along the way.

Wranglers looked after the *remuda*. A remuda was a group of extra horses that replaced tired horses on the trail.

wrangler with remuda

The cook drove the **chuck wagon** ahead of the herd, so he could prepare food for the cowboys when they arrived.

chuck wagon

drag riders

flank rider

swing rider

trail boss

Flank riders rode beside the herd. They kept the cattle from spreading out too far.

flank riders

point rider

Drag riders rode behind the cattle and other cowboys. They kept the herd moving.

Swing riders turned the herd in the right direction.

Point riders rode in front of the herd. They led the cattle and other cowboys.

The **trail boss** was in charge of the trail drive. He rode ahead of the herd to find a place to camp. He also kept track of how many animals were lost during the drive.

The chuck wagon was like a traveling kitchen.

The cook drove from a bench at the front of the wagon.

The **chuck box** held food, utensils, and other supplies.

A coffee grinder, tin cups, pots, and pans hung from nails or hooks on the outside of the chuck box.

The back of the chuck box folded down into a table. The cook prepared the meals on this table.

The **boot** was a box under the wagon. It held pots and pans.

A barrel of fresh water was attached to the side of the wagon.

Iron bars were laid across a fire pit to make a cooking surface.

After a hard day on the trail, cowboys relaxed by the campfire. They told stories, sang songs, and played harmonicas and guitars.

Beans with beef was a cowboy's main meal.

bread

A **dutch oven** was used to make pies, biscuits, bread, and beans. To cook food evenly, hot coals were placed all around this iron pot.

Most trail drives headed east to cattle towns in Missouri and Kansas. Some went north to Canada.

Wagon trains

Cowboys were not the only people who traveled to the West. Many families also moved west to build homes on their own land. They traveled in **covered wagons**, which carried their belongings. Groups of families traveled together so they could help one another. A line of covered wagons traveling together was called a **wagon train**. The travelers in a wagon train faced many dangers, such as heat, cold, disease, and attacks by wild animals. They also had to travel through dangerous storms, such as the one shown below.

covered wagon

Wagon trains traveled in long lines across the plains.

Many travelers died in deadly storms.

Men hunted animals such as wild turkeys and pheasants. The food was cooked over a fire.

Each covered wagon
was loaded with a
family's belongings.
Name all the things
you see in this wagon.

At night, the wagons stopped and formed a circle
for protection. People put up tents inside the circle.
They made fires for cooking and to keep warm.

The Gold Rush

In the mid 1800s, gold was discovered in the rivers of the West. Thousands of people traveled west to find their fortunes. This great movement of people was called the **Gold Rush**. The people who traveled west in search of gold were known as **prospectors**. Anyone who arrived at the **gold fields** had a chance of "striking gold." At first, prospectors looked for gold in rivers. Soon, many prospectors became **miners**. Miners dug into the ground to find gold buried deep in rocks. There were several gold rushes, bringing many people to different parts of the West.

Miners often worked together to search for buried gold.

covered wagon

pick

Prospectors traveled long distances in search of gold.

18

Many miners used pans to separate gold from dirt. Some "panned for gold" day after day.

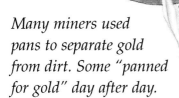

handle

sieve

gold

Gold was sometimes separated in a **cradle**. Dirt was shoveled onto a metal **sieve**, and water was poured over it. The handle rocked the sieve, washing the dirt out the end. The gold stayed in the cradle.

dirt and water

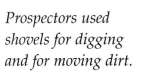

Prospectors used shovels for digging and for moving dirt.

A **pick** loosened and broke away pieces of rock.

sluice

A **sluice** was used to wash large amounts of gold. The gold fell into the **riffles**, or ridges, and the dirt was washed out at the end. Large sluices could wash gold as fast as two or three people could, who were using pans.

riffles

shovel

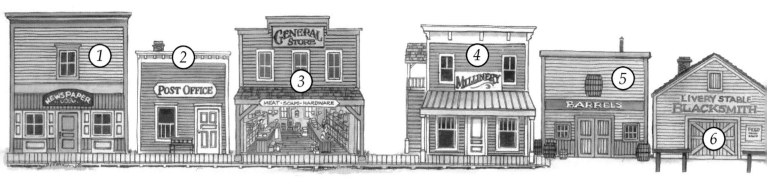

Boomtowns

As more and more settlers arrived, **boomtowns** sprang up all over the West. A boomtown is a community that grows very quickly. People built houses and started businesses in their communities. Boomtowns attracted many **merchants**, or store owners. They sold goods in shops. People who offered **services** also set up businesses. Services provided work or help for money. Hotels and restaurants are examples of services. **Trades** opened shops, too. Trades were skilled workers, such as blacksmiths, who made or repaired things. Make a list of the businesses you see at the top and bottom of these pages. Which were merchants? Which offered services? Which were trades? Which were more than one kind of business?

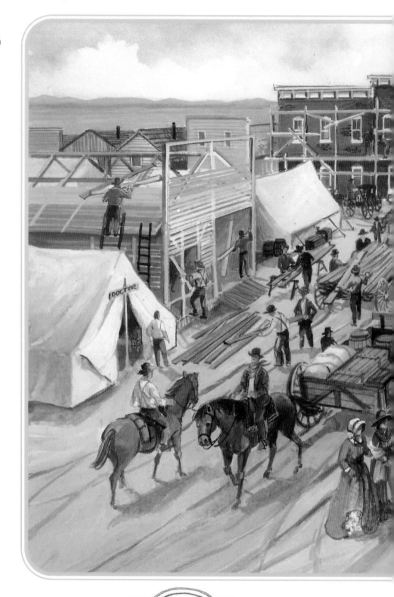

(7) WAGON REPAIR
(8) REAL ESTATE / LAND CLAIMS
(9) UNDERTAKER
(10) DOCTOR / DENTIST
(11) CITY HALL

GENERAL STORE
LAW OFFICE

Answers:
merchants: 3, 4, 19
services: 1, 2, 8, 9, 10, 11, 13, 14, 15, 16, 18, 20, 21
trades: 5, 6, 7, 9, 12, 17, 19

(17) CARPENTER
(18) INSURANCE
(19) BOOTS SHOES
(20) SALOON
(21) SHERIFF'S OFFICE

Law in the West

The West soon became known as the "Wild West." There were very few law officers, and most people carried guns. Men who worked hard all day looking for gold often spent their evenings drinking in **saloons**, or taverns. Many fights broke out, and people were hurt. Robberies were also a big problem in the West. Some people robbed banks, and others robbed stagecoaches. Some found ways to cheat people out of gold by making dishonest business deals. Danger lurked around every corner!

stagecoach

WANTED

Dalton "Babyface" Fast

$5,000 REWARD

Notify AUTHORITIES

Some criminals went from town to town, robbing banks and other businesses.

Other criminals robbed stagecoaches. Stagecoaches carried bank money, as well as passengers.

sheriff

*In early boomtowns, the sheriff was the only protection against criminals. Many sheriffs took **bribes**, however. They were criminals, too! In later days, laws were passed, and police officers patrolled the streets.*

Mounties

In 1873, the Canadian government hired 300 police officers to form the North West Mounted Police, also known as the Mounties. The Mounties brought law, order, and justice to the lawless Canadian West. They also stopped criminals from crossing the border and smuggling whiskey. Criminals were afraid of the Mounties!

Early western homes

Settlers had to build shelters or homes as soon as they arrived in the West. In the plains, the land was mostly flat, and there were few trees for building homes. The only material for building was **sod**. Sod was soil with grass growing on it. Settlers cut bricks of sod from the ground and piled them up to make their homes. They used mud to keep the bricks together. To make roofs for their homes, settlers placed sod over wooden frames.

dugout roof

*Some settlers built **dugouts** when they first arrived in the West. They dug out the sides of hills to make caves and made the front walls from sod. Animals sometimes fell through the roofs of their homes!*

wooden frame

sod bricks

People who settled in the plains built sod homes like this one.

well

bucket

log home

In areas with many trees, settlers could build log homes. Log homes were safer and cleaner than sod homes were. To make log homes, settlers stripped the bark from logs and then **squared** the logs.

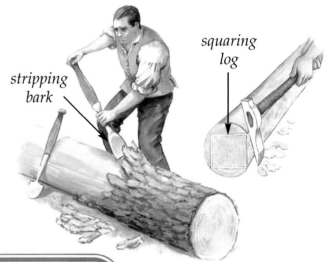

stripping bark

squaring log

Settlers could not live without water! Some people built homes near rivers or lakes, but most people had to dig wells to get water. This mother is using a bucket to pull up water from a well for her thirsty children.

adobe

Settlers in the Southwest used adobe bricks to make their homes. Adobe was a mixture of clay, sand, straw, and water that became very hard when it dried. Settlers stacked adobe bricks to make thick walls. They then spread a mixture of clay and water over the walls to make them look smooth.

Helping one another

journal

When settlers arrived in the West, they found that most of the land was wilderness. Those who lived on the plains had to build sod homes because there were no trees. They also had to plant crops quickly so they would have food to eat. Living on the plains was very lonely. The next neighbor was often several hours away! When people did find neighbors, they helped one another as much as they could. Men worked together building homes, schools, and churches. They helped one another dig wells. Women held **bees**, or work parties, to make quilts or to preserve food for the winter.

*Some women wrote letters or kept **journals**, or diaries. They had few books, which they read over and over again.*

bales of hay

*Children were very happy when they could meet and play with other children. While their parents were **harvesting**, or cutting down, hay for animals to eat, the children enjoyed games of hide-and-seek among the **bales** of hay. Bales are bundles that are wrapped tightly so they can be carried and stored.*

Women sometimes gathered together to do jobs such as sewing, knitting, and quilting. Having company made the work a lot more fun. These women are at a quilting bee. They are sewing a quilt on a quilting frame.

In later times, families and friends visited one another on Sundays and on special holidays. They dressed in their best clothes for these special occasions. Sometimes they had their pictures taken by photographers.

Trains bring new settlers

Travel to the West was dangerous and took a long time. Then railways were built, and the West changed forever. People from all over the world could travel to the West and start new lives. Traveling by train was quicker, safer, and more comfortable than traveling by wagon train. The railroad also carried goods from east to west. People in the West could now buy all kinds of items from other parts of the country. The railroad provided thousands of people with work, as well. Most important of all, the railroad linked the country from coast to coast. It helped create new towns and cities.

Thousands of people worked on building train tracks. **Graders** *prepared the ground to make the land flat.* **Ties** *were then laid on the ground. Heavy iron* **rails** *were placed over the ties and nailed down with big metal* **rail spikes**.

rail spikes

A steam locomotive

The locomotive pulled the other rail cars. It was at the front of the train.

*The **smokestack** allowed smoke to escape from the firebox.*

*The **boiler** was filled with water. Water was heated until it became steam.*

*Steam traveled to **cylinders**. It moved the **pistons** inside. The pistons turned the **driving wheels**.*

*Wood was heated in the **firebox**.*

firebox

piston

cylinder

driving wheel

Flares were placed on tracks to warn trains to slow down or to stop.

Flags were like traffic lights. What do these colors mean?

stop

slow down

train whistle

oil lamp

Cowcatchers *pushed animals off the tracks.*

first-class car

People who wanted to travel by train could travel in first-class, second-class, or third-class passenger cars. First-class was very comfortable and served meals.

Homes of the wealthy

Businesses grew quickly in the West. Many people became very wealthy. They wanted to have the same kind of luxury as the people in eastern North America had.

Many wealthy westerners built large Victorian homes, such as this one. These fancy homes were painted in bright colors and were called "painted ladies." On the outside, they were decorated with **gables** and **turrets**. On the inside, Victorian homes were just as beautiful.

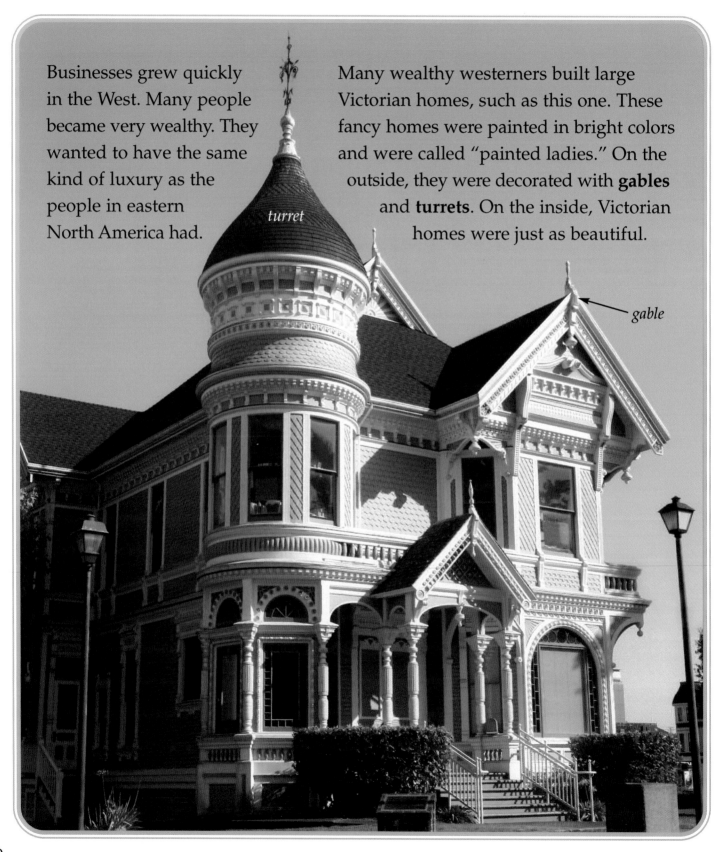

turret

gable

Many Victorian homes had libraries filled with expensive leather-bound books.

The most formal room of the house was the **parlor**. It was also known as the **salon** or **drawing room**. The parlor was used only for entertaining guests or for Sunday family gatherings.

Hand-painted oil lamps were used to light the rooms in Victorian homes.

washstand

pitcher

wash basin

chamber pot

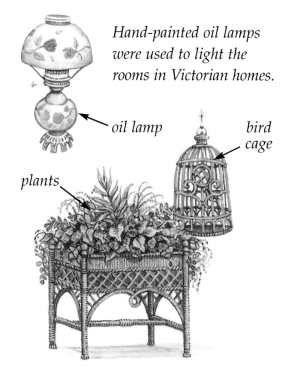

oil lamp

plants

bird cage

Washstands were kept in the bedrooms. They contained pitchers and wash basins. **Chamber pots** were built into chairs and served as indoor toilets.

Some houses had **conservatories**, or greenhouses. Plants, fountains, and caged birds made these rooms feel like the outdoors.

Glossary

Note: Many boldfaced words are defined where they appear in the book or are shown by pictures that are labeled

breaking Taming a horse so it can be ridden

bribe Money taken by a law officer to ignore an illegal act

bunkhouse A place where workers lived

conservatory A room with glass walls

corral A fenced area where horses are kept

gold fields Areas where gold was found

grader A worker who makes roads flat

harvesting Cutting and gathering ripe crops

hide The skin of an animal that is prepared and used to make clothing, blankets, or tents

journal A book in which daily events and feelings about those events are written down

mission A religious community that tries to change the beliefs of people who live there

native nation A group of people who lived in North America before others arrived and who spoke their own language and had their own customs and traditions

permanent Meant to last for a long time

plain A large area of flat land with few trees

prospector A person who looks for gold

saloon A place where alcoholic drinks are sold and drunk

service The action of doing work, such as cutting hair, or helping others for money

settle To make a home in an area where few other people lived

sieve A utensil for straining liquids and catching solid particles

stable A barn where horses are kept

stagecoach A closed horsedrawn wagon that carried passengers, mail, and often, money

Index